The UNITED STATES
in the COLD WAR

1945–1989

The UNITED STATES
in the COLD WAR

1945–1989

Christopher Collier
James Lincoln Collier

BENCHMARK BOOKS

MARSHALL CAVENDISH
NEW YORK

ACKNOWLEDGMENT: The authors wish to thank Tom Paterson, Professor Emeritus, University of Connecticut, for his careful reading of the text of this volume of The Drama of American History and his thoughtful and useful comments. The work has been much improved by Professor Paterson's notes. The authors are deeply in his debt, but, of course, assume full responsibility for the substance of the work, including any errors that may appear.

Photo research by James Lincoln Collier.

COVER PHOTO: *Corbis*

PICTURE CREDITS: The photographs in this book are used by permission and through the courtesy of: *Corbis:* 12, 14, 22, 25, 28, 31, 33, 37, 42, 45 (bottom), 50, 55, 58, 60, 62, 64, 66, 72, 74, 75, 84, 86; *Library of Congress:* 11; *National Archive:* 44; *NASA:* 52 (bottom); *New York Public Library:* 10, 13, 18, 19, 30, 52 (top), 83; *U. S. Center of Military History:* 45 (top), 69, 73, 78, 80.

Benchmark Books
Marshall Cavendish Corporation
99 White Plains Road
Tarrytown, New York 10591-9001

©2002 Christopher Collier and James Lincoln Collier

Library of Congress Cataloging-in-Publication Data

Collier, Christopher, (date)
    The United States in the Cold War / Christopher Collier and James Lincoln Collier.
       p. cm. — (The drama of American history)
    Includes bibliographical references and index.
    ISBN 0-7614-1317-0
    1. United States—History—1945—Juvenile literature. 2. United
States—Foreign relations—1945-1989—Juvenile literature. 3. Cold War—Juvenile
literature. [1. United States—History—1945- 2. United States—Foreign relations—
1945-1989. 3. Cold War.]   I. Collier, James Lincoln, (date) II. Title.

E741 .C537 2001
327.73'009'045—dc21   00-068010

Printed in Italy

1 3 5 6 4 2

CONTENTS

PREFACE

Over many years of both teaching and writing for students at all levels, from grammar school to graduate school, it has been borne in on us that many, if not most, American history textbooks suffer from trying to include everything of any moment in the history of the nation. Students become lost in a swamp of factual information, and as a consequence lose track of how those facts fit together and why they are significant and relevant to the world today.

In this series, our effort has been to strip the vast amount of available detail down to a central core. Our aim is to draw in bold strokes, providing enough information, but no more than is necessary, to bring out the basic themes of the American story, and what they mean to us now. We believe that it is surely more important for students to grasp the underlying concepts and ideas that emerge from the movement of history, than to memorize an array of facts and figures.

The difference between this series and many standard texts lies in what has been left out. We are convinced that students will better remember the important themes if they are not buried under a heap of names, dates, and places.

In this sense, our primary goal is what might be called citizenship education. We think it is critically important for America as a nation and Americans as individuals to understand the origins and workings of the public institutions that are central to American society. We have asked ourselves again and again what is most important for citizens of our democracy to know so they can most effectively make the system work for them and the nation. For this reason, we have focused on political and institutional history, leaving social and cultural history less well developed.

This series is divided into volumes that move chronologically through the American story. Each is built around a single topic, such as the Pilgrims, the Constitutional Convention, or immigration. Each volume has been written so that it can stand alone, for students who wish to research a given topic. As a consequence, in many cases material from previous volumes is repeated, usually in abbreviated form, to set the topic in its historical context. That is to say, students of the Constitutional Convention must be given some idea of relations with England, and why the Revolution was fought, even though the material was covered in detail in a previous volume. Readers should find that each volume tells an entire story that can be read with or without reference to other volumes.

Despite our belief that it is of the first importance to outline sharply basic concepts and generalizations, we have not neglected the great dramas of American history. The stories that will hold the attention of students are here, and we believe they will help the concepts they illustrate to stick in their minds. We think, for example, that knowing of Abraham Baldwin's brave and dramatic decision to vote with the small states at the Constitutional Convention will bring alive the Connecticut Compromise, out of which grew the American Senate.

Each of these volumes has been read by esteemed specialists in its particular topic; we have benefited from their comments.

CHAPTER I

The Causes of the Cold War

In history we very often see events caused by well-meaning people doing things that seem right at the time, but unhappily lead to tragedy. Such was the case with the Cold War between the United States and the USSR: Both sides thought they were doing the right thing, but in the end it brought death and destruction to millions of people.

The Cold War—a term in wide use as early as 1949—ran from the end of World War II to 1989, when the Communist system in Russia collapsed. Put in the simplest terms, the Cold War was a standoff between the two dominant powers in the world. Because both Russia and the United States had huge stockpiles of nuclear weapons, enough to destroy much of human civilization, they were deterred from starting a real—or "hot"—war between them. But neither could they find ways to live in peace and harmony with each other. Indeed, instead of engaging in good-faith negotiations, they often engaged in propaganda wars over the virtues of capitalism and communism.

In the years since the First World War the original Russia had swallowed up most of the small surrounding lands, like the Ukraine to the west, Kazakhstan to the south, Lithuania to the north, and many more.

By the end of World War II these had been welded into one great nation, dominated by the Russians: the Union of Soviet Socialist Republics—called the USSR, or the Soviet Union. But many of the peoples of the lands in the USSR continued to speak their own languages and follow their own folkways; they often felt more like captive nations than equal members of a great union. (In this volume we shall use the term *USSR*, or *Soviet Union*, for the period between 1918 and 1989; otherwise we shall use *Russia*.)

How, then, did these two wartime allies against Hitler become enemies? In order to understand why, we need to try to look with a clear,

The Soviet Union drew—or forced—into it many small nations that had not yet been industrialized and were still peasant cultures. From the start the Soviet Union was thus well behind the other industrialized nations. These crockery menders in the fabled city of Samarkand in Uzbekistan, were at the time of the Russian Revolution still using bow drills in their repair work.

objective eye at two emotionally charged words: *capitalism* and *communism*. We have a tendency in America today to see capitalism as all good and communism as all evil, but as is usually the case, the story is not quite that simple.

Historians have traced the roots of capitalism quite far back in time, but it clearly was in existence by the 1500s. Before, and indeed for a long time afterward, most people in Europe and elsewhere lived as peasants on land owned by very wealthy aristocrats, like dukes, princes, earls.

However, a few people were finding ways to *invest* money by, for example, buying up a lot of wool, having it woven into cloth, and selling the cloth at home or abroad for a profit. Others invested in ships going out to Africa, Asia, the Americas, to bring back spices, furs, ivory, which could be sold at home for great profits—if the ships did not sink in storms. Still others invested in mines and the machines to work them.

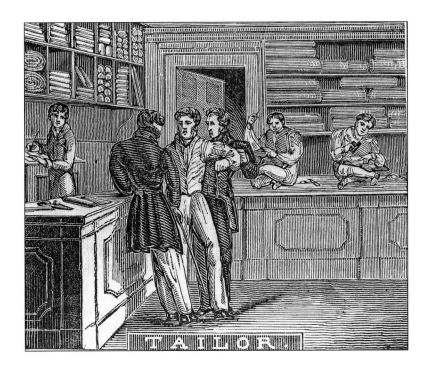

The first capitalists were usually small businessmen, like this tailor with a few employees, who invested money in cloth, thread, needles, and rent in hopes of making a profit.

Not all of these investments were profitable, but many were. These profits could be used to make even larger investments. The money thus piled up—money used to make more money—was called *capital,* and the system of investment was called *capitalism.* This early capitalism made a few people well-to-do, and a tiny handful rich.

In the 1800s, particularly in the United States and Europe, a sudden shower of inventions and technological improvements made it possible to make goods faster and cheaper than by hand. Many new types of goods that had never been seen before, like telephones and electric engines, appeared. To profit from a new idea, the inventor had to get capital from investors to build the factories and machines which would produce his new product. The investors would, of course, own the factories, machines, railroads, iron-ore mines. (Nineteenth-century technology and industry have been described in the volumes in this series called *Andrew Jackson's America* and *The Rise of Industry.*)

Over time, machinery replaced manual labor. The first factories in the United States and many places elsewhere were driven by water-power. By the mid-1800s steam engines were creating much more efficient and much larger factories; and by the end of the century electric power was making even larger and more efficient factories possible.

New farm machines made it possible for fewer people to grow more crops, more livestock. Millions of people were forced, or chose, to move into rapidly growing cities to work in factories, on railroads, in mines, instead of plowing and haying in the countryside. Life for millions of humans changed. (The story of this urban migration is told in the volume in this series called *The Rise of the Cities.*)

In capitalism, the idea was—and is—to make the largest amount of profit possible. One way to increase profits is to cut wages. Capitalists in the new industrial nations were often able to keep wages very low, because jobs were often scarce, and many people competed for them. As a consequence, most working people were badly paid and suffered from poor living conditions—eating cheap and often unhealthy food, sometimes going hungry, and living in squalid, overcrowded apartments and shacks.

Some people benefited. "White collar" workers in company offices, or owners of small businesses, earned much more money than laborers, and could live comfortably. And the investors, a tiny percentage of people, often got rich, although of course an investment was always a risk, and many lost their money.

It is true that the system raised the level of living for almost everyone. It is also true that entrepreneurs and their investors created jobs by building new factories, opening new mines; profits had to be large to encourage people with money to risk it. But the cost was high, for most of the laborers worked ten or twelve hours a day under hard and often unsafe conditions for wages that barely fed and clothed their families.

As early as the 1830s many people, especially in Western Europe, were beginning to believe that there was something wrong with the capitalist system, which forced the majority of people to live desperate lives in squalor. Workers organized themselves into unions and struck for higher wages. Sometimes these efforts succeeded; more often they did not, or at best improved things only a little.

In order to increase profits, mill owners tried to keep wages as low as possible. They often employed children, who were paid less than adults. Children were particularly useful in textile mills, because their smaller fingers were better at knotting threads. But even by the early years of the 1800s many people were objecting to the harshness of life for factory workers and to the use of child labor, as this political cartoon shows. The man with the stick is saying, "Why did you let go the spindle you young villain?" The girl replies, "My fingers were so cold I could not hold it. Oh dear, pray do not kill me. Oh my back! Oh dear! Pray forgive me."

Soon philosophers, historians, and frequently the workers themselves began to develop new ideas of government that would modify the capitalist system, or even get rid of it altogether. There were a great variety of these new philosophies of government—socialism, anarchism, and more. These philosophies, which aimed at restricting or replacing capitalism, have generally been called "left wing," because their adherents sat on the left side of the French national legislature. There were many differences among them, but in the main they favored the rights of working people against the capitalists. In fact, today much of what these left-wingers wanted in the nineteenth century is thoroughly accepted, including government pensions for the elderly, medical insurance, unemployment benefits, free education for all. But in the nineteenth century, especially in the United States, left-wing ideas seemed radical.

Among these left-wing philosophies was communism, developed by two Germans, Karl Marx and Friedrich Engels, who put forth their ideas in a series of books and pamphlets written in the mid-1800s. Communist theory is complicated and sometimes contradictory. Basically, it said that the "means of production"— factories, mines, railroads—ought to belong to the people who worked them, not the capitalist investors. In time, Marx and Engels believed, the workers in various nations would revolt, take over their governments, and join together in a great peaceful international world order. Eventually it would not even be necessary to have a government: The workers, through their committees in the factories and elsewhere, would make such decisions as had to be made, and government would "whither away."

Karl Marx wrote one of the most famous works of modern times— Das Kapital (Capitalism)—in which he urged workers to rebel against the hard conditions of industry and form their own Communist states.

Whether communism, as envisioned by Marx and Engels, would have worked in practice is a question. The odd fact is that although many nations eventually called themselves communist, none of them really put all of the Marxist ideas into practice: Marxism as Marx envisioned it has never really been tried.

Whatever the case, it is easy to understand why capitalist investors, small-business people, and the middle class in general, most of whom were earning comfortable salaries working in corporations, were utterly opposed to communism. Should communism ever come, they would lose everything (including their lives in too many cases, as happened in the USSR). It is also easy to understand why many working people were attracted to communism and left-wing ideas generally, which promised them more power and better lives. Particularly in Europe, Socialist and Communist political parties gained some power, although they never truly became dominant anywhere except for brief periods.

But neither communism nor socialism ever attracted large followings in the United States. Far fewer than 1 percent of Americans ever joined the Communist Party even at its peak during the Great Depression in the 1930s. Why were American laborers less attracted to communism than Europeans? Partly it was because many of the left-wing ideas that had been worked out in Europe were brought to the United States by immigrants, and seemed to many Americans "foreign ideas." For another reason, the newspapers, and later radio and television, which are, after all, owned by capitalists, were resolutely opposed to communism. They rarely could find anything good to say about communism and the left wing in general, always depicting them as "menaces." Perhaps more fundamentally, American working men aspired to rise into the middle class and perhaps become capitalists themselves—which some did. The main point for us to bear in mind is that when communism arose as an actual force in the world, rather than a theory, Americans were already predisposed to fear and hate it as a worse threat to them than it actually was.

In 1914 World War I began, with Britain, France, and Russia allied against Germany and other nations. The war went badly for Russia. The nation was a monarchy, ruled by a czar and wealthy aristocrats, with the huge mass of the people working in dire conditions on vast agricultural estates or in factories in big cities. The Russian people wanted to get out of the war in which their sons, husbands, and fathers were being slaughtered by the tens of thousands. A revolt brewed, and in 1917 a new, mainly democratic, government took over. However, it did not immediately withdraw Russia from the war. The Communists saw their chance, and with the help of soldiers and workers in St. Petersburg, then the Russian capital, ousted the democratic government, quickly made a separate peace with Germany, and began organizing the large Russian nation into a Communist system.

Inevitably, many people in the Western nations were alarmed—indeed frightened—by the rise of communism in Russia. They reasoned that if it could happen there, it could happen anywhere, even in the United States, in which case businessmen large and small, white-collar workers, and owners of stocks and bonds would lose everything. As we have seen, these fears were exaggerated: There was no chance of a Communist takeover in America, and a not much greater one in Europe. But the fear was there, and the United States joined with several European nations and Japan in sending troops into Russia to aid some Russians who were fighting the new Communist government there. This effort failed: The Communists had much support from the Russian people, who had suffered under the czars and were ready for a change. In the end the United States refused to send an ambassador to Russia, although most other nations did. (The great "Red Scare" of the 1920s is described in the volume in this series called *Progressivism, the Depression and the New Deal*.)

Understandably, the Russian leader, Vladimir Lenin, quickly came to believe that his country was now surrounded by enemies determined to

This highly romanticized painting of Lenin was typical of Russian art under the Soviets. In reality, Lenin was a ruthless manipulator, but nonetheless a remarkable leader, who established the Soviet Union in the face of many difficulties.

bring down his government. (His fears were grounded in history: Russia's vast open plains on both its eastern and western borders had been invaded over and over by such enemies as the Mongols in Asia and Napoleon's troops on the west.) We can see, thus, that as early as 1920 the new Union of Soviet Socialist Republics and the United States were already hostile to each other.

This fear of encirclement alone might have caused Lenin to employ ruthless means, but he was going in that direction anyway. Lenin and the other leaders believed that nobody should be allowed to stand in the way of "the dictatorship of the people": Enemies should be removed—by a firing squad if necessary. For the good of the workers, the Communist government must be all-powerful; there would be in the Soviet Union no supreme individual rights like freedom of religion, speech, or assembly. This was bad enough, but in 1924 Lenin died, and the government was taken over by Joseph Stalin, who was not merely ruthless but one of the worst tyrants in human history, although this was not apparent for some time. Stalin demanded absolute power; he put into office only those who kowtowed to him, and executed without remorse any who stood in his way. According to Marxist theory, control should lie in the hands of the workers through their committees; according to Stalin, control lay at the top. Among other things, the peasants, whom Lenin had freed from the big estate owners, were now forced back onto "collective farms," huge ventures controlled from Moscow. In the end, Stalin ordered the execution of thousands of his own people. Agricultural and industrial policies he decreed led to the death by starvation of millions more. By the 1930s Stalin's control was complete.

Thus, although Americans had, at this time, little to *fear* directly from Communist Russia, there was much to hate about it. And yet, despite everything, some good did come out of the Soviet Union. By the 1930s the majority of Russians were better off than they had been under the czars. The country was being industrialized; people who had never had shoes now wore them. Huge housing projects replaced many slums. People's diets improved. Things were unquestionably better, although the USSR never achieved the kind of prosperity that people in the Western democracies took for granted. And of course political freedoms, including a meaningful vote, were almost entirely absent. Indeed, there was only one political party to vote for.

We must remember that in the years leading up to World War II the world, in particular Europe and America, was suffering through the terrible Great Depression. Some people who visited the Soviet Union and saw the improvement communism had brought to many people there thought that it might be the answer to problems elsewhere. Communist parties grew up in many Western nations. In France, Spain, and a few other places, they played a significant role in government at times. But for the most part these Communist parties were too small to be effective, and were controlled by Moscow for the purposes of the USSR.

This was especially true in the United States. The Communist Party had always been quite weak there: In 1932, at the bottom of the Depression, the Communist candidate for president drew only a quarter of 1 percent of the vote, some 100,000 people, about as many as can fit into a large football stadium. And by the start of World War II in 1939, Americans were, in general, strongly anti-Communist in feeling. A collision might have been expected.

The Soviet Union never did catch up to the United States in industrial power, but it made enormous strides. Compare this 1949 scene with the earlier picture of the crockery menders of thirty years before.

CHAPTER II

The Cold War Begins

Events in Europe delayed the collision between the USSR and the democratic nations. In the 1920s and 1930s fascist governments arose in Germany, Italy, Spain and elsewhere. By the mid-1930s the German leader, Adolf Hitler, was demanding—and taking—some of the lands around Germany. War seemed in the offing. Stalin made a peace treaty with Hitler in order to stave off an invasion, though he knew that Hitler would eventually attack. In 1939 World War II began, with England and France poised against Germany and Italy. Soon Hitler broke the peace treaty and invaded the Soviet Union. Americans wanted to stay out of the war, but in 1941 the Japanese, allied with Hitler, attacked the American naval base at Pearl Harbor in Hawaii; the United States was in the war. The United States and the USSR were now allies. The U.S. government and the press had to persuade the public that Stalin was not so bad after all, and got some Americans to think of him as a kindly "Uncle Joe"; communism was seen to be at least preferable to fascism. (The story of the war is told in the volume in this series called *The United States in World War II*.)

During the war the Allied leaders, President Franklin D. Roosevelt,

Three of the greatest men of the twentieth century at a meeting in the Soviet city of Yalta during the last years of World War II: British prime minister Winston Churchill, U.S. president Franklin D. Roosevelt, and Soviet dictator Joseph Stalin. At this meeting they divided Europe in two, with the Soviets to control the eastern portion, the democracies the western section.

Joseph Stalin, and the British prime minister, Winston Churchill, met at various times to make war plans. By 1944, although there would be hard fighting ahead, it was clear that the Allies would win. The leaders decided to meet to plan for the peace. A conference was arranged to take place near the city of Yalta in the Russian Crimea in February 1945.

Of particular concern to all three leaders were the lands lying more or less between the Soviet Union and Germany—what are now Poland, the Czech Republic, Slovakia, the Balkans, and Hitler's allies Hungary, Bulgaria, and Austria in particular. Roosevelt wanted to see these nations guaranteed democratically elected leaders so their citizens could shape their own governments. Stalin, however, had other ideas. Whatever he said, he believed that the Soviet Union needed to have on its borders countries sympathetic to communism, not capitalist democracies allied against communism with the United States, England, and others. And he was in a position to get what he wanted, because by the time of the Yalta Conference, Soviet troops were chasing the Germans out of these Eastern and Central European nations and taking charge there.

Later some people said that in agreeing to let the Soviets have control in the area east of Germany, Roosevelt had "sold out" the nations there. However, most historians believe that Roosevelt had simply been facing reality: The Soviets already had their troops, tanks, aircraft in those places and couldn't be simply ordered out. They had, after all, suffered over twenty million deaths at the hands of Hitler and his allies; Stalin looked for revenge.

In April 1945, a sick and weary Franklin Roosevelt died. He was succeeded by Vice President Harry S. Truman, who had served in France as an artillery officer during the First World War and was, for many years, a senator from Missouri. Truman was a self-made man, more rough and tumble than the aristocratic Roosevelt, but nonetheless intelligent, honest, and surprisingly shrewd in his judgments of people. For a while after his presidency, many considered him a mediocre leader, but by the end of the twentieth century, historians saw him as unusually clearheaded, decisive, and possessed of sound judgment.

In early May 1945, the fighting ended in Europe. The Soviet army was now well into Germany and occupied its capital, Berlin. In August 1945, the American military exploded two atomic bombs in Japan, destroying the cities of Hiroshima and Nagasaki. (For a discussion of the decision to drop the atomic bomb, readers can see *The United States in World War II*.)

World War II was now over. The wartime alliance between the United States and the USSR was ended. Inevitably, old attitudes resurfaced. Stalin continued to believe that at bottom, the Western democracies were hostile to communism, which was undoubtedly true, and might well attack him, which was probably not true. In fact, both sides were mistaken in their judgments of the other. Americans believed that the Soviet

Union possessed a powerful military force, partly because of its victories over Germany, and partly because Soviet propaganda said so. In truth, the Soviet Union was devastated, its economy a wreck, many of its cities in ruins, twenty-three million dead. It was in no position to fight another war.

The United States was. During the war it had built a mighty fighting machine, and the nation, untouched at home by any fighting, was prosperous. Above all, the United States alone possessed the atomic bomb. Stalin could see all this. But he did not grasp that in a democracy, public opinion was paramount, and in 1945 the American public, sick of war, sick of seeing its young men die in strange lands they had never heard of, would not have stood for another war unless there were desperate reasons for it. The United States was not going to start fighting again to keep the Soviets out of, let us say, Poland. What mattered, however, was not the reality, but how things were perceived to be. Both sides grew fearful seeing the other as a bully.

In July 1945, the leaders had yet another meeting, this time at Potsdam, a suburb of Berlin. At first President Harry Truman decided that he liked Stalin: "He is honest—but smart as hell," he said. Very quickly he changed his mind: The Soviets were "pigheaded" and "were planning world conquest." There was some reason for believing this. Communists had always said that "history was on their side," that the triumph of communism was inevitable, and that the Soviets would certainly support and encourage Communist revolutions wherever they could. But there was a misperception here, too: While the Soviets might well have welcomed Communist revolutions, they were hardly in a position to think about conquering the world, or any significant portion of it.

The big problem confronting the Allied leaders at Potsdam was what to do about Germany. The nation was in ruins. Originally, many people thought that Germany, which had started two world wars in a generation, ought to be stripped of its industry and turned into an agricultural nation incapable of fighting another war. Stalin, in addition, wanted "reparations," that is to say, payments from Germany for the damage its armies had done in the USSR. He would get this in the form of German machines, indeed whole factories, with which to rebuild ruined Soviet industry.

But by the time of the Potsdam Conference, the American, British, and French leaders had decided that Germany, once the most powerful industrial nation in Europe, had to be rebuilt. They were beginning to fear that the Soviets would exploit the economic devastation in not only Germany but much of Western Europe, and support Communist takeovers there. A strong Germany might act as a buffer against the Soviets.

By the time the war was winding down in the summer of 1945, Roosevelt had died, and Harry S. Truman had become president. Churchill had been voted out of office in favor of Clement Attlee. Only Stalin remained. He agreed to allow free elections in the Eastern European nations under his control, but Truman did not trust him—correctly, as it turned out.

It also seemed to the American, British, and French leaders that Europe could not be rebuilt as an industrial force under a capitalist system without a strong Germany at its heart. However, Germany would not be allowed to rebuild its war machine; defensive forces against a Soviet attack would be provided by the Allies, particularly the United States.

In the final Potsdam agreement, Germany was divided into zones, with the Soviets controlling the eastern part, the British, French, and Americans controlling the west and south. Berlin was in the Soviet zone,

The Post-War Division of Germany into Zones

but it was also to be cut up into zones shared by the Allies. The Soviets would be allowed moderate reparations in the form of machinery. The Soviets also reaffirmed their agreement to allow free elections in some of the places under their control, Poland in particular.

Very quickly, however, Stalin showed that he was not going to abide by the agreements unless forced to. The Soviets began stripping their zone of machinery as fast as they could, along with a lot of art, gold, and other valuables. By 1947 they had installed puppet governments in Poland, Hungary, Romania, and Bulgaria, where their troops were in control. The USSR refused to move its troops from oil-rich Iran on its borders, despite having agreed to do so. The United States and the USSR struggled to gain political influence there. Finally the United States gained the support of the Shah, and the Soviets concluded a treaty with Iran and left.

The Americans, however, still hoped that a better spirit between the two powerful wartime Allies could be maintained. The United States offered to reveal the secrets of the atomic bomb to everybody if control of the world's atomic energy was given to the United Nations, which could work out a system for limiting, or eliminating, atomic weapons. The Soviets, who were trying to develop their own atomic weapons, insisted that the Americans should turn over the secrets before controls were set up. The Americans refused. Realistically, the old alliance was dead. Early in 1946, when the war had not yet been over for a year, Stalin made a speech in which he said that war between communism and capitalism was inevitable. A month later Winston Churchill, in another famous speech, warned that the USSR was dropping an "iron curtain" across Europe.

It seemed clear that the USSR was going to expand wherever it could. In February 1946, George Kennan, an American diplomat in Moscow, sent a long, secret telegram to Washington saying that the USSR was going to push outward. America must institute "a long-term, patient, but firm and vigilant containment of Russian expansive tendencies." The

Stalin soon installed puppet governments in the Eastern nations, such as Czechoslovakia, Poland, and Hungary. In 1956 some Hungarians started a revolt against their puppet government. At left, a truckload of freedom fighters rolls into the Hungarian capital of Budapest. But Stalin quickly responded with force. Below, Russian tanks stand guard on a street in Budapest. The rebels were beaten by superior might, and other of the captive nations took notice.

telegram was taken seriously by President Truman and his advisers. It became the basis for the policy of *containment* of the Soviet Union specifically, and communism in general.

The policy was soon acted upon. In March 1947 there was growing turmoil in Greece and Turkey. Poverty and chaos beset both countries. In Greece, a Communist-led civil war was under way. Truman was fearful

Eastern Block

FINLAND

NORWAY   SWEDEN

Tallinn
ESTONIA

North Sea

DENMARK   LATVIA
              Riga   U.S.S.R.
        Baltic
        Sea   LITHUANIA
                Vilnius

NETHERLANDS

                POLAND
          Berlin   Warsaw
        EAST GERMANY

BELGIUM

WEST GERMANY
          Prague
        CZECHOSLOVAKIA

FRANCE

        AUSTRIA

SWITZERLAND   Budapest

                HUNGARY

                        ROMANIA

                        Bucharest
                YUGOSLAVIA   Black
                                          Sea
        ITALY   BULGARIA
                                Sofia

        Mediterranean   GREECE
            Sea   ALBANIA

SCALE of MILES
0   100   200   300

N

that the Soviets would seize the opening, step into the chaos, and take over both Greece and Turkey. He delivered a speech to Congress saying that the world was now divided between nations "based on the will of the majority," and those relying on "terror and repression." The United States must "support free peoples who are resisting attempted subjugation by armed minorities or by outside pressure." What he meant by this "Truman Doctrine," really, was that attempts by Communists to take over anywhere, either from outside or inside of a nation would be resisted by the United States. The policy of containment of the USSR was now being put into practice.

Once again, the danger of Communist takeovers in Turkey and Greece were considerably less than Truman said; some people believe that he exaggerated the Communist threat in order to get Congress to

In 1947 turmoil in Greece worried President Truman. He thought that Communists controlled by Stalin might take over there. Truman proclaimed what came to be called The Truman Doctrine, which said that the United States must face down the threat of Communist takeovers wherever they occurred. This idea of "containing" communism became basic to American foreign policy. Here Greek troops prepare to fight Communist rebels. An American adviser stands at right rear.

authorize the new policy of containment. Whatever the case, the Cold War had clearly begun.

With the example of Greece before them, the Americans came to believe that the post-war poverty and turmoil in Europe might open doors to communism. Desperate people often make desperate choices: Hitler had risen to power in Germany, in 1933 when the German economy seemed to have broken down. To lessen the chance of such economic chaos, Truman's government worked out the so-called Marshall Plan, first outlined by Secretary of State George C. Marshall, who had been army chief of staff during the war. Under the Marshall Plan the United States sent over twelve billion dollars—in addition to nine billion already spent there—in aid to Western European nations, including Germany, to help them rebuild their economies. The importance of the Marshall Plan was enormous, for it was critical in making Western Europe the economic power it eventually became.

Secretary of State George C. Marshall testifies before Congress during the crisis in Greece. Marshall, who had been Chief of Staff during World War II, devised the so-called Marshall Plan, to lift a broken Europe back into economic health as a way to forestall communist influence.

The Marshall Plan was also offered to the Eastern nations that were under Soviet control, but the Soviets refused to permit them to accept American aid. However, in 1948 the Czechs, still free from Soviet control, considered accepting Marshall Plan help. The Soviet army supported a Communist coup and installed a puppet government in Prague. In the course of this takeover the Czech leader, Jan Masaryk, died suspiciously.

Germany was even more of a tinderbox. The Soviets had fairly thoroughly looted the eastern sector of the old Germany. Berlin, an island in the Soviet zone, was still shared with the Western powers. As it became clear that the Soviets would probably not agree to the establishment of a United Germany along the lines of the old one, the Americans, French, and British combined their territories into a West German republic. In May 1948, Stalin responded by blockading the movement of supplies from the West into the Allied sector of Berlin, hoping to starve the Western Allies out. Truman responded by creating a gigantic airlift; in ten months American pilots flew in 2.3 million tons of supplies to soldiers and civilians in the West Berlin zone. In June 1949, Stalin gave up and called off the blockade. Soon the Soviets turned their zone into the German Democratic Republic, with a Communist government controlled from Moscow. Germany was now divided into two separate nations: one Communist-controlled, one a capitalist democracy tightly allied with the West. Berlin remained a divided city, a small Western enclave surrounded by Communist East Germany. The Iron Curtain ran through the middle of Germany.

There now existed, in effect, an alliance of the nations of Western Europe with the United States. It was understood that in case of a Soviet invasion of Western Europe, the Americans would have to supply much of the defense. In April 1949, twelve Western European nations signed an agreement establishing the North Atlantic Treaty Organization, called NATO, which continues to exist today, though much enlarged and including some nations formerly controlled by the USSR. The treaty

When the Soviets cut off American access to Berlin, hoping to starve Berliners into submission, Truman started a huge airlift to bring food and supplies into the beleaguered city. Here, Berlin children wave to an American plane coming in with food.

pledged all of its nations to defend any that were attacked, which meant effectively that the United States would defend Western Europe against a Soviet attack. (In 1955 the Soviets organized a counterbalancing organization, known as the Warsaw Pact, although in fact the Soviets already controlled the nations involved.)

The last step in this division of Europe came in 1961. Thousands of East Germans had regularly been escaping into the West, despite barbed wire and machine guns, both across the line dividing the two Germanys, and the line dividing Berlin. Suddenly, on the night of August 13, 1961, the East Germans laid down a barbed-wire barrier. They followed this

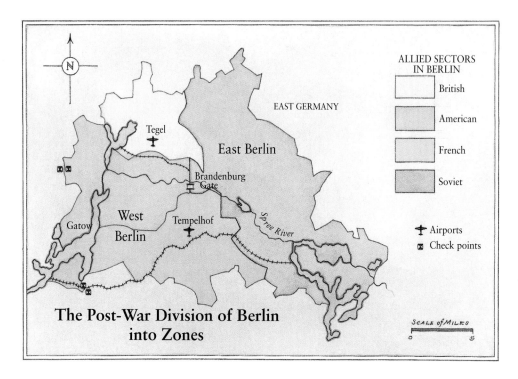

The Post-War Division of Berlin into Zones

ALLIED SECTORS
IN BERLIN

British

American

French

Soviet

✝ Airports

☒ Check points

EAST GERMANY

East Berlin

Tegel

Brandenburg Gate

West Berlin

Tempelhof

Gatow

Spree River

SCALE of MILES
0   5

quickly by a tall cement block wall cutting Berlin in half, making escape virtually impossible. The wall would stand as the most visible symbol of the Cold War for twenty-eight years.

World War II had only been over for four years when NATO was formed in 1949, and it had only been fifteen years since Hitler had begun grabbing up lands belonging to Germany's neighbors. Fresh in everybody's mind was the fact that the democracies, especially England and France, had failed to stop Hitler when a strong show of will would have done it. The success of the Berlin airlift seemed also to show that only firm dealings by the Western nations would hold off the Soviet Union. Most Americans believed that it, like Germany under Hitler, would expand in all directions if not stopped. By 1949 the alliance of Western nations had blocked Soviet expansion in Europe; soon all eyes would be on Asia.

Once again, on both continents, the Cold War was being fueled by misperceptions. The United States and its allies had no intention of invading the Soviet Union, or even preventing the Soviets from establishing puppet states, like Poland and East Germany, where they were already in effective control. It was equally true that, while the USSR would like to have seen Communist governments in France and West Germany, there was little they could, or would, do about it. Both sides had less to fear from the other than they believed, but it was the belief in these exaggerated fears that determined the course of history.

CHAPTER III

The Cold War Spreads to Asia

The United States had long held friendly feelings toward China. Americans had been sending their ships across the Pacific to trade with the Chinese for tea, silk, "Chinaware," and much else, almost from the moment the American nation was formed. In the 1800s, Chinese religious ideas were studied by American philosophers, and many American churches established missions in China, converting thousands—though a tiny minority—of Chinese to Christianity.

In the 1920s China was nominally ruled by the Nationalist Party led by Jiang Jieshi (formerly spelled Chiang Kai-shek). He was a Christian, his wife had gone to college in the United States, and they were popular with Americans. Nonetheless, the Nationalist government of Jiang Jieshi was corrupt and inefficient. Millions of Chinese farmers struggled in poverty against overbearing landlords. In the 1920s a Communist leader, Mao Zedong, began to attract followers. By the 1930s the Communists were in rebellion against the Nationalist government and had gained control of sections of China.

In December 1945, a few months after the war against Japan was over, President Truman sent General George C. Marshall to China to

A thoughtful Mao Zedong in a portrait from about 1970. As leader of the Chinese Communists, he was one of the most important figures of the twentieth century. As this picture shows, he had a philosophic turn of mind, but he was also ruthless in seeking his goals.

negotiate a peace between Jiang Jieshi's Nationalists and Mao Zedong's Communists. The peace failed to hold, and in 1949 the Communists won. Jiang Jieshi and his followers fled to Taiwan (then called Formosa), a group of islands off the southeast coast of China.

Many Americans, both in and out of government, had strongly supported Jiang Jieshi, despite the corruption of his government. They were incensed, and accused Marshall and the Truman administration of "losing" China. Indeed, some claimed that unnamed Communists in the American State Department had deliberately undercut Jiang. Among the most notorious of these accusers was Senator Joseph McCarthy, who, in order to promote his own political career through the early 1950s, made a series of spectacular charges that the State Department was riddled with Communists. He never offered any proof, and was later completely discredited, but at the time, his charges were widely believed. (The story of McCarthyism is told in the volume in this series called *The Politics of Prosperity*.)

Historians today agree that the United States could not have prevented the Communist takeover of China, short of mounting an all-out war there, which the American people would never have supported. They also believe that there were few, if any, Communists in the State Department. But the Democrat Truman grew sensitive to Republican charges that he

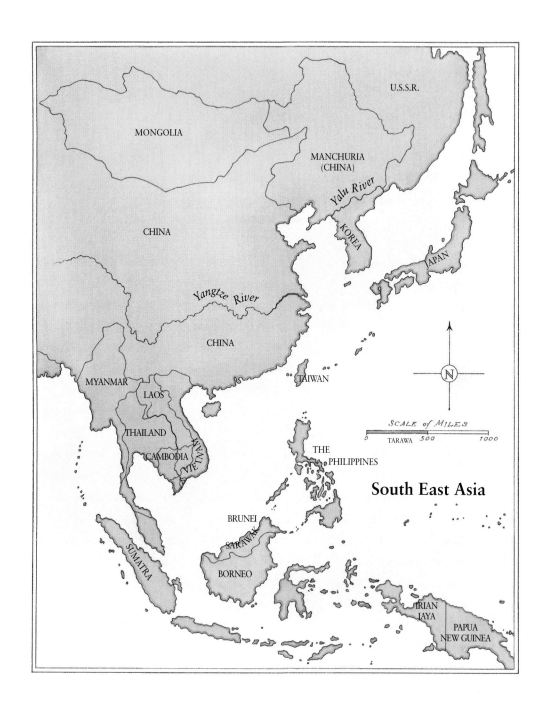

Mongolia
U.S.S.R.
Manchuria (China)
Yalu River
China
Korea
Japan
Yangtze River
China
Taiwan
Myanmar
Laos
Thailand
Cambodia
Vietnam
N
SCALE OF MILES
0   TARAWA   500   1000
The Philippines

South East Asia

Brunei
Sarawak
Sumatra
Borneo
Irian Jaya
Papua New Guinea

might be "soft on communism." Truman refused to recognize China's Communist government, foreclosing any chance for open diplomacy with Mao Zedong.

Events were now unfolding more rapidly than anyone expected. The nation of Korea, a peninsula descending south of China, had long been under Japanese control. As World War II was winding down, with Japan prostrate and China in the midst of its civil war, the Soviets sent troops into Korea. The Americans quickly sent in troops of their own and soon what was supposed to be only a temporary dividing line was established at the 38th parallel. In their northern sector of Korea the Russians put in charge a Korean who had spent World War II in the USSR, Kim Il Sung. In the south, Syngman Rhee, who lived in the United States for thirty years, took over, with American protection. Both Rhee and Kim insisted that they intended to unify Korea under their own governments, by force if necessary, and indeed border skirmishes became common.

With the help of the USSR, North Korea built up its military forces. The Americans, tired of war, and with their military drastically reduced from its World War II peak, in an effort to discourage Rhee's aggression did not supply South Korea with much military equipment. With support from both the USSR and Mao Zedong's Chinese government, North Korea felt emboldened. And, in fact, remarks made by the American secretary of state seemed to suggest that the United States considered the peninsula outside its area of "containment" and would not fight to defend South Korea. In June 1950 the North Koreans swept across the 38th parallel, driving the thin South Korean forces before them.

President Truman was now faced with a tough decision. On the one hand, Americans, after ten years of the Depression and four years of war, were finally having prosperous times. Further, the great military machine built during World War II had been largely dismantled. The country was not ready for another war. On the other hand, Truman was committed to a policy of the containment of communism. McCarthyite extreme

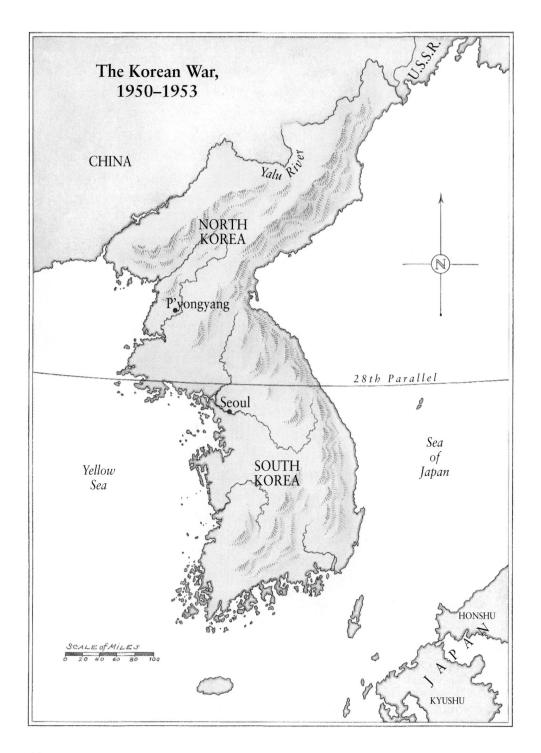

The Korean War,
1950–1953

CHINA

Yalu River

U.S.S.R.

NORTH
KOREA

N

P'yongyang

28th Parallel

Seoul

Yellow
Sea

SOUTH
KOREA

Sea
of
Japan

SCALE of MILES

0 20 40 60 80 100

HONSHU

JAPAN

KYUSHU

anticommunism had great influence within the Republican Party, and the Democratic president did not want to appear afraid to stand up to the Communists. Additionally, the North Koreans were clearly the aggressors. Finally, there remained in everybody's minds the appeasement of Hitler in the late 1930s, which had led to the horrors of World War II. Truman said, "Communism was acting in Korea just as Hitler . . . had acted . . . . If we let Korea down, the Soviets will keep right on going . . . . " He decided to act.

But he did not want to make it solely an American war. He urged the United Nations to take action. The UN Security Council quickly demanded that the North Koreans withdraw, which of course they did not do. Truman now had a second problem. According to the Constitution, the president cannot go to war on his own say-so: Only Congress can declare war. This rule had been got around before and has been since by other presidents. Truman argued that since the United Nations had urged its members to furnish help to beleaguered South Korea, and since the United States was a member of the UN, he, as U.S. commander in chief, was authorized to send troops into combat without congressional approval. He immediately ordered the American navy and air force to help the South Koreans. The North Koreans pressed on, taking the South Korean capital city, Seoul. Truman then ordered American troops stationed in Japan flown to Korea. Five years after the end of World War II the United States was at war again—though an undeclared one.

Technically, then, it was not a war but a "police action" of the United Nations. In fact, although other countries sent token forces to Korea, almost all of the non-Korean troops were American, the bulk of the supplies came from America, the top generals were American, and the cost was mainly paid by American taxpayers. It was an American war, fought to uphold the American policy of the containment of communism.

The American intervention in Korea raised constitutional questions that would come up again and again during the Cold War. At the time

American troops search a Korean village for North Korean guerrillas. During the early days of the fighting, the Americans took severe losses.

the United Nations was formed, Congress passed laws saying that the president could lend troops to UN actions, provided that Congress had agreed in advance to the particular type of action it would support. Congress, however, had not worked out any such agreements. In sending troops to Korea, Truman was certainly stretching the Constitution, if not actually breaking it. Truman had felt that there was no time for a lengthy debate over the "police action," and Congress, generally supportive of the policy of containment, did not challenge him.

General Douglas MacArthur, who had led American forces against Japan in the Pacific during World War II, was put in charge of UN forces in Korea. By August 6, 1950, hardly two months after their attack, the North Koreans had swept all the way down the peninsula. The Americans and South Koreans clung grimly onto a small corner around the city of Pusan.

As routine military planning, the Defense Department had already worked out a scheme for just such a situation: The defenders would make an amphibious landing well up the Korean Peninsula, behind the battle line at the city of Inchon. MacArthur quickly seized on this idea. On September 15, a force of U.S. marines landed at Inchon and drove inland. The North Koreans fled in disorder, and very quickly MacArthur's troops were driving them back north.

Now there was another decision to be made. The original UN resolution called only for pushing the North Koreans back behind the 38th parallel, the original dividing line. It now looked as if UN forces could sweep into North Korea, pull down the Communist government, and unite the two Koreas. The big question was: What would Korean's northern neighbor, China, with a vast nation of more than 500 million people, do?

Douglas MacArthur had always seen himself as a man of destiny and liked to exercise a theatrical flair. As head of American occupation forces in Japan he ruled that nation almost as his private kingdom. He was also, for various reasons, strongly opposed to communism. In the back of his mind he hoped to push the United States into a war with China to put an end to communism there.

MacArthur then advised Truman that the Chinese would not intervene if the Americans pushed into North Korea, despite the fact that the Chinese had strongly suggested that they would. Truman and his advisers decided to allow MacArthur to go northward, provided he stay well back of the Yalu River, which divided Korea from China. Nobody consulted the United Nations, although this was officially a UN fight. MacArthur pushed his troops forward until they were very close to the Yalu River, in disobedience of his orders. Late in October, Chinese troops began to fight alongside the North Koreans. Then, on November 26, Chinese troops poured across the Yalu and began driving the Americans and South Koreans back again.

The battles that followed made what had gone before seem like child's play. The Chinese forces were not nearly as well equipped as the Americans, but their leaders had an enormous supply of troops, all close at hand. Their most effective battle tactic was to throw hordes of soldiers at the Americans, the later ones climbing over the bodies of their dead companions to get at the American lines.

Furthermore, the countryside where much of the fighting was done was rough mountain territory, bitterly cold during the winter months. Wounded Americans often froze to death lying in trucks on the way to hospital tents. Men fought with their feet and hands frozen, their faces encrusted with frost. Struggling to stay warm in foxholes at night, they slept only fitfully, fearful of Chinese infiltrators striking a bayonet into

The undermanned American troops were driven out of the South Korean capital of Seoul right at the beginning, but then fought their way back in as reinforcements arrived. Here, American troops in a shoot-out during street fighting in Seoul.

Above: A combat artist's painting of an American truck column held up by cannon fire hitting the road ahead of them. Combat artists, themselves soldiers, made quick sketches of the action and then completed the painting later.

Right: An American machine gun emplacement. Much of the fighting took place in the mountains in bitter cold, which added to the soldiers' misery.

them. The Americans, overwhelmed by numbers, fought furiously but were driven back along winding mountain roads, shelled from above as they went.

In one typical battle, Private Herbert K. Pililaau, fighting at the infamous Heartbreak Ridge, volunteered to cover a retreat of his company from the ridge with his machine gun. As his comrades slipped away, Pililaau fired at the enemy until his ammunition was exhausted. He then fought them off with grenades. Finally, as the rest of the company watched from below, he fought the onrushing enemy with his trench knife. Said one of his buddies, "There was Herb standing up fighting a lot of the enemy. We wanted to go back up to help him but the captain said, 'No.' We tried to help Herb by firing a few shots, but they didn't do any good. All of a sudden they shot him and when he went down they bayoneted him. That was it." Forty dead Chinese were found around Pililaau's body when his unit retook the hill. Herb Pililaau was awarded the Medal of Honor.

Eventually the UN forces regrouped, counterattacked, and pushed the enemy back. By spring 1951 the front line had stabilized at about the 38th parallel. But MacArthur was no longer in charge. He had too often ignored instructions from Washington, and was now urging a war against China, maybe even using atomic weapons. MacArthur was very popular with Americans and Truman hesitated to discipline him. But then, as Truman was trying to work out a peace treaty, MacArthur, implying that Truman was an appeaser, publicly threatened to expand the war into China, something he had no authority to suggest. Truman, commander in chief and embodiment of the principle of civilian rule of the military, relieved him of his command.

In 1952 a Republican, the World War II hero General Dwight "Ike" Eisenhower, became president. Negotiations with the Chinese had been going on, but they had stalled. In his election campaign Eisenhower had promised to "go to Korea" to see if he could end the war. After he

In the 1952 election campaign General Dwight Eisenhower announced that he would go to Korea to seek peace. Right after the election he did so. Here (left), he eats with a group of soldiers near the front lines.

became president he secretly let the Chinese know that he might use "tactical" atomic weapons against them—that is, no bombs that could blow up whole cities, but smaller ones against troops. Diplomacy, of course, was complicated by the fact that the United States still had not recognized the Chinese Communist government. The Chinese decided to give way on some disputed points, and in July 1953, delayed for months over how to deal with thousands of Korean prisoners of war, an armistice was signed. Things were now back to where they had been in June 1950, when the North Koreans had first attacked.

The Korean War was very costly in human life. Two million North Korean *civilians* and a half-million North Korean soldiers died. The South

Koreans lost a million civilians and 47,000 soldiers. The United States had 54,000 dead, more than died in combat in World War I. The Chinese reported 148,000 dead, but the true figure was undoubtedly much higher. Many Korean cities, towns, and villages were devastated; many farms ruined. The war cost Americans twenty billion dollars as well.

Did the Korean War accomplish anything? It showed, certainly, that the United States was willing to fight to contain communism. It was clear, for example, that the United States would step in if the Soviets tried to move into Western Europe.

It showed, also, that a group of nations could work together under a common institution, in this case the United Nations. This had never been done before.

But it was also clear that American leaders had made a huge mistake in crossing the 38th parallel instead of ending the war there as was originally planned. Perhaps misled by MacArthur, the temptation to bring down a Communist nation had been too great to resist. Threatened, the Chinese came in, and millions of lives were lost.

CHAPTER IV

The Arms Race and the Third World

The world now appeared to be divided into two camps: on one side the Western democracies and Japan; on the other side the Soviet Union and its Communist allies. In fact, as ever, the picture was not that simple. For one thing, as we shall see, there were a great many countries around the world that did not belong to either camp, and did not want to. For a second, as we shall also see, the Communist nations were by no means unified. There was, for example, much friction between The People's Republic of China and the Soviet Union, with at times open hostility. Communist Yugoslavia resolutely refused to knuckle under to the USSR. But more and more Americans, and many others, came to see the world as polarized: It was us against them.

Among those who thought that way were President Dwight Eisenhower and his influential secretary of state, John Foster Dulles. Dulles, indeed, had participated in the American intervention in Russia against the Communists in 1918. Communism was philosophically opposed to religion. Many religious people saw it as especially evil, as an enemy, even, of God. Dulles was the son of Christian missionaries, and saw communism as not merely a political or military threat to the United

John Foster Dulles, secretary of state under Dwight Eisenhower, brought an almost religious fervor to the battle against communism. He found it very difficult to find ways to compromise on this issue.

States, but almost the voice of the devil that ought to be crushed for that reason alone. Dulles was not alone; many others in the United States and elsewhere thought this way. Such people brought to the Cold War a crusading fervor: Communism must be stopped at almost any cost. Eisenhower tended to agree, but he knew war, and always wanted to avoid it.

It is nonetheless true that Communist governments were almost always totalitarian dictatorships in which opposition to the government was ruthlessly crushed, political enemies were tortured, sent to forced labor camps, or simply executed. Under Soviet-style communism, people had few freedoms, and lived regimented lives controlled by distant bureaucrats in faraway cities. Thus, it was not easy for Americans, or anyone else for that matter, to maintain a balanced, objective view of the Communist nations; far easier to see them as the evil enemy, and that is what most Americans, including government officials, did. Of course, there was always a faction that saw the matter differently. There were those—some in government—who thought that American fears were exaggerated and urged a more compromising diplomacy.

The United States had begun to rebuild its war machine during the Korean War, but Eisenhower wanted to run a financially conservative government—to "get a bigger bang for a buck," as Dulles put it. The most practical course, then, was to develop a system by which the United States would threaten other nations with a show of atomic—or as they are now called, nuclear—weapons. The United States stationed bombers in England, from where they could carry nuclear weapons to Soviet cities. But it was also clear that missiles that could deliver nuclear warheads to the enemy from a great distance would be better than bombers. By the 1950s both sides were working frantically to develop nuclear missiles.

In 1953 Joseph Stalin died. After a struggle for power among Stalin's subordinates, he was succeeded by Nikita Khrushchev, a rough, roly-poly man with an outgoing personality who was nonetheless as tough as nails. Khrushchev soon revealed to the Soviet people, and the rest of the world as well, that Stalin had been responsible for the death of millions of Soviet citizens, as well as other crimes. It appeared that he might be less cruel than Stalin. Nevertheless, Khrushchev pushed Soviet interests as hard as ever, once telling an American president, "We will crush you."

Then, in August 1957, Khrushchev announced that the Soviets had fired an *intercontinental ballistic missile* (ICBM)—that is, a missile that could fly from one continent to another carrying a nuclear weapon. Two months later the Soviets launched *Sputnik*, the world's first space satellite.

It appeared that the Soviet Union was moving ahead of the United States in technology, especially weapons technology. Since at least World War II, the United States had considered itself the world's leader in technology and was stunned, indeed horrified, by these Soviet triumphs. Congress hastily passed laws promoting the teaching of science in high schools and colleges, and supporting scientific research. Very soon the United States had its own ICBMs. Nonetheless, there was a lot of talk about the "missile gap," suggesting that the Soviets had more, and better, ICBMs.

In fact, they did not. President Eisenhower had information—gathered by American spy planes—that the United States was not behind the

Left: The Soviets scored a great propaganda success with the launching of their ICBM and soon after, Sputnik space satellite. They also were ahead of the Americans in putting a man into space. This illustration from the Soviet magazine Krokodil shows Yuri A. Gagarin, the space hero, being celebrated by Russian citizens. In fact, the Soviet lead in missiles was not nearly so great as Americans feared.

Right: The American effort to put a man on the moon was as much for propaganda as for any practical purpose. This famous photo was shown worldwide. It was now clear that the Americans had regained the lead in space technology.

Soviets in missile technology, but was well ahead. However, he did not want to reveal this for fear that there would then be pressure to cut back government spending on missile research and manufacture. The American public grew fearful of a nuclear bomb attack. Many Americans built bomb shelters in their backyards that they stocked with supplies of food and water. Schools held air-raid drills in which students were taught to hide under their desks during an attack. Many Americans who turned fifty in 2000 still recalled with dread those frightening elementary school air raid drills.

The arms race was truly on. Each side felt it had to keep up with the other in missiles. In the end, both nations would have enough missiles equipped with nuclear weapons to end life on this planet. Both Eisenhower and Khrushchev, no matter what they thought of each other, realized that neither country could start throwing nuclear weapons at the other without being sure of getting the same back. Technically, it was simply not possible for one side to take out all of the other's missiles in a surprise attack. The two camps had achieved "mutually assured destruction," or the "balance of terror," as some put it. In a nuclear war, both countries would be destroyed. The two leaders tried to be conciliatory, and in 1955 Khrushchev made a trip to the United States, where he visited Disneyland, but also had long serious talks with Eisenhower.

The contest between the two great powers was not, however, just over missiles. Communism, we remember, was an international movement; its goal had always been to create Communist nations everywhere—indeed, a Communist world. Similarly, America had always felt that its interests would be best served by the building of democracies, which also seemed to most Americans a blessing for the people concerned. Both nations, thus, began courting other nations around the world, in hopes of bringing them into their own camp.

There existed a great many "developing" nations, those only partially industrialized (or, indeed, hardly industrialized at all) and whose people were quite poor, badly educated, without good medical care, and frequently beset by civil war and famine, as they still are today. Most of these countries are in the southern half of the world, and are racially non-white; that is, African, Asian, Arab. Some of these nations had once been colonies of the European powers, seen as sources of raw materials, and had never developed much industry. Others had clung to traditional peasant farms or even nomadic life. Many of these nations had come to be ruled by despots of one kind or another, sometimes hereditary kings, sometimes strongmen with the support of the local army. These despots were usually surrounded by a small group of followers who owned vast properties from which they grew immensely rich—rubber, sugar, cotton plantations, timberlands, mountains rich in minerals. Ordinary people in such nations were virtually serfs, living in poverty and despair. It is not surprising, then, that there were revolutionists among them. (These are sometimes called "Third World" nations; the United States, the Soviet Union, and their allies being first and second worlds.)

It is very important for us, at this point, to grasp the idea that there is a difference between *communism* and the *Soviet Union*. At the time, a great many people, including presidents, failed to understand it. Whatever the Soviets wanted people to think, they were actually far more interested in doing what was good for the USSR than in spreading communism. For example, when the Chinese Communists made it clear that they were not going to take orders from Moscow, the Soviets quickly stopped supporting them.

Conversely, many smaller nations interested in the Communist philosophy did not believe they had to always follow the Soviet lead. Not only China, but Communist Yugoslavia, Communist Albania, and others actually split with the Soviet Union to go their own separate ways. But most Americans, and unfortunately many people in government, including both Eisenhower and Dulles, did not really understand this.

Going a step further, people did not understand that all revolutions in

Yugoslav dictator Tito (left), whose real name was Josip Broz, was just one of several Communist leaders who resisted control by the Soviets. Here he is shown at the air-port in the Yugoslav capital, Belgrade, with Soviet premier Kruschchev. It is significant that Khrushchev paid a visit to Tito rather than demanding that the Yugoslav leader come to Moscow.

developing, or Third World, nations were not fomented by Communists. Some were dominated by Communists, some were not. Many of these revolutionary movements were "wars of national liberation" against European imperialist domination. Since these European nations, like France, were Cold War allies of the United States, American officials thought they had to support them against the local revolutionaries. Making it more complicated, at times and places Communist and non-Communist leaders might be struggling for control of the revolutionary movement themselves. It is no wonder that the American people found it difficult to follow the ins and outs of politics in the developing nations. But of course it was the job of government officials to understand these differences.

Many lower officials and experts did. Unfortunately, there was a ten-dency of presidents and their advisers to believe that if a nation, or its leaders, was not with the United States it was against it. Eisenhower and Dulles certainly thought that way. There was no understanding that a developing nation might be neutral in the Cold War. In practice, this meant that a developing nation had to follow American policy if it wanted American financial and military aid. In particular, they had to be anti-Communist.

Despots in nations like Cuba, Guatemala, the Philippines, and elsewhere understood this. In exchange for huge amounts of American aid, they tried to squelch communist sentiment among their people; often they allowed Americans to establish military bases in their countries. Regrettably, many of these despots and their wealthy allies managed to put much of the American aid in their own pockets, instead of seeing that it benefited their people, as it was meant to do. American officials often knew this, but they believed it was worth it to keep such nations from "going communist"—even when there was no good evidence that they might.

The final result was that when conventional peasant revolutions broke out in such countries, Americans often could not see that the revolutionaries had very real grievances. Government officials tended to smell Communist influence in any revolution—and indeed there often was. So the United States, a country founded in revolution and always dedicated to national self-determination and democracy, again and again found itself supporting despots in order to "fight communism." And when these revolutions succeeded, as they sometimes did, American governments tended to remain suspicious of their governments if they tried to remain neutral in the Cold War.

Americans had a second problem with these revolutionary governments. Many, if not most, of them had risen to power on a policy of land redistribution—that is, the large plantations, ranches, and timberlands owned by a handful of the very rich would be divided up among the peasants who did the work on them. Many of these plantations actually belonged to American and European companies. For example, the famous U.S.-based United Fruit Company owned huge banana plantations in Central America and had always been very powerful there.

According to international law, these corporations still owned these lands. Revolutionary governments often took them, anyway. This frontal attack on private property and capitalist principles was a sore point with the American government.

It has to be realized that the Soviet Union was also deeply involved in the Third World—encouraging revolution, promoting communism, attempting to control rebellions when they occurred. The Soviet Union had less compunction than the Americans did about murder and torture, although it is true that some American agencies, especially the oft-criticized Central Intelligence Agency (CIA), did secretly resort to assassination a few times. Like the United States, the Soviet Union offered aid only with the understanding that the client nation would follow its policies on important issues.

A case in point is Egypt. In 1952 the corrupt Egyptian king, Farouk, was swept aside by some army officers led by Gamal Abdel Nasser. Nasser promised to distribute land to small farmers and to end British control of the Suez Canal. Nasser also tried to forge alliances with other Arab nations, in part to fend off the influence of the Cold Warriors. As ever, Secretary of State Dulles was suspicious of Nasser's attempts to stay neutral in the Cold War, by making deals with either side as it suited Egypt's interests. Nonetheless, Dulles promised American money for the building of the huge Aswan Dam on the Nile. At the same time, Nasser entered into an agreement with some other Arab nations that seemed to be aimed at Israel. Israel was in the American camp. Next, Nasser made a deal with Soviet-controlled Czechoslovakia for weapons. Soon afterward Egypt recognized Communist China. Dulles believed that Nasser was thinking about joining the Soviet camp, and withdrew the offer of aid for the Aswan Dam. The Soviets immediately offered Egypt the money for the dam. Soviet money inevitably carried Soviet influence. Nasser built the dam and also wrested the Suez Canal from British control.

To be sure, Nasser was not naive: He had been cleverly playing the

The Middle East

SCALE of MILES

0   500   1000

The United States originally promised to help the Egyptians build the huge Aswan Dam, but backed off when they suspected Egyptian leader Gamal Nasser of working with the Soviets. Eventually the Soviet government helped to pay for the dam.

superpowers off against each other, as many of the Third World countries were learning to do. Still, American leaders feared that a nation that would not follow American policy on major issues was flirting with communism.

Egypt, however important to the United States, was a good distance away from America. Cuba, on the other hand, was only ninety miles from Florida. The island nation had always been dominated by American individuals and companies who controlled sugar plantations, cattle ranches, and other businesses there. As was so often the case, the American government supported the Cuban strongman, Fulgencio Batista, a typical despot supported by a small minority of the rich and powerful. Batista had enriched himself through a system of payoffs and bribes. In late 1956 a young Cuban lawyer named Fidel Castro started a rebellion from a base in the mountains. He quickly attracted much support from a wide spectrum of Cubans. Although many Americans sympathized with Castro and his rebellion—indeed, for a while he was a popular hero in the United States—the United States government was worried that he might open the way for a communist Cuba, once again without much evidence either way.

In January 1959 Castro drove Batista out and began taking over sugar plantations and mines, some of them belonging to American citizens. Castro also executed some of Batista's supporters, and ejected some of the American military people who had helped Batista's army against him.

It is understandable that Fidel Castro would have had no love for the United States, which had supported his enemy Batista. And by taking control of American-owned lands, which he did not distribute to the peasants but kept under his government's control, he knew he would anger the American government. A more conciliatory person might have found ways to accomplish his goals and still maintain a friendly relationship with the United States. But Castro was determined to undo a half century of American domination of Cuba. (American influence in

Cuban rebel Fidel Castro proved to be a flamboyant personality, but he could keep the Cuban economy afloat only with the help of the Soviets. He is seen here at a press conference in Havana in 1959, shortly after he took control of Cuba.

Cuba is described in the volume in this series called *The United States Enters the World Stage.*)

But it is also true that Eisenhower, Dulles, and many other Americans were, almost by instinct, hostile to revolutions, particularly in this case, where American business interests had been damaged. The United States government made little effort to work out a relationship with Castro, but marked him down as an enemy. In March 1960, Castro signed a trade treaty with the Soviet Union. Soon the American government cut off trade with Cuba, hoping to hurt its economy, especially by cutting off sales of Cuban sugar to the United States. The idea was that if the Cuban economy collapsed, Castro might be overthrown. President Eisenhower also decided to train anti-Castro Cuban exiles, many of them former supporters of Batista, for an invasion of Cuba.

Then Eisenhower's term of office ran out and John F. Kennedy became president. The Cuban exiles training in Florida were under the control of the CIA. President Kennedy had a lot of doubts about the invasion of Cuba. However, the CIA assured him that the Cuban people were

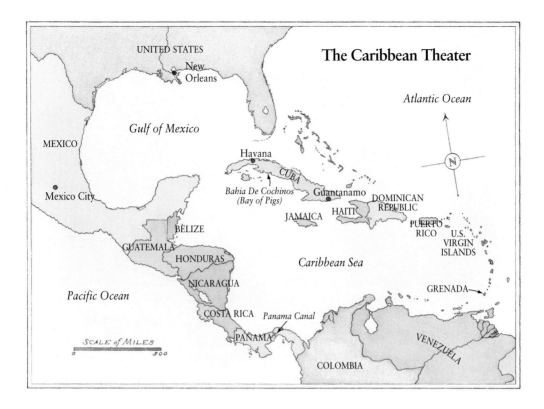

The Caribbean Theater

fed up with Castro and would rise against him when the invasion started.

On April 17, 1961, 1,453 Cuban rebels invaded at a place called the Bay of Pigs (Bahía de Cochinos). The Cuban people did not rise against Castro, and the invasion was quickly squelched. The Kennedy administration was badly embarrassed and began looking for a way to get rid of Castro, by assassination if necessary. Inevitably, Castro looked more and more to the Soviet Union for support. In time, Soviet financial aid became essential to the Cuban economy.

In addition, Moscow sent Cuba jet planes, patrol boats, and much else to protect it against an expected American invasion, that it knew John Kennedy was considering. The Soviets also sent missiles to Cuba, some with nuclear warheads that could reach parts of the United States.

The United States discovered these missiles in October 1962. For several days President Kennedy agonized: He was determined to get the missiles out of Cuba, but he was not sure whether to invade, bomb the mis-

At left, a group of Cuban exiles in training to mount an invasion of their homeland against Castro. They believed that once their small force landed, the Cuban people would rise up in support of them, and they persuaded President Kennedy to let them go ahead. Below, somber members of the Bay of Pigs invading force are marched into one of Castro's jails. The Cuban people did not rise to support them, and Castro had an easy time putting the invasion down.

sile sites, or try to negotiate. In the end he went on television, told the American people about the missiles and said he was going to blockade Cuba to prevent arms shipments already on the way from the USSR. Hotheads on both sides were itching for a fight: The world was on the precipice of a nuclear holocaust. Kennedy and Khrushchev were eyeball to eyeball. Who would blink? Both leaders remained cool and eventually worked out a deal in which Khrushchev would withdraw some missiles from Cuba if the United States would take away some missiles it had in Turkey, close to the Soviet border—although to make Kennedy look good, this part of the deal remained secret for a while. Kennedy also made an implicit promise not to invade Cuba.

The Cuban missile crisis scared people enough so that a "hotline" was set up for quick communication between the Soviet and American leaders. The two superpowers also began negotiating controls of nuclear weapons. We shall hear more about that shortly.

Despite everything, the United States and Cuba remained enemies until the end of the twentieth century, and beyond. Some historians today believe that had American leaders been more tolerant of Castro, who could not, after all, have mounted a serious threat to the United States, he might not have turned to the Soviets for support, and Cuba would perhaps be a more democratic nation than it is. (Despite all this, strange as it may seem, the United States kept its naval base at Guantánamo Bay on the eastern end of the island of Cuba, still there in the year 2000.)

Unfortunately, the tendency of American leaders to suspect that Communists were behind any sort of revolution, and to support cruel and corrupt despots in order to "fight communism," badly hurt the reputation of the United States, not only in the Third World, but in Europe as well. Tens of millions of people concluded that there was little to choose from between the United States and the USSR: Both seemed to be dominating bullies. These people lost sight of the fact that America was the most prosperous, and perhaps politically the freest nation in the

After the missile crisis the United States continued to keep a close watch on ships going into Cuba. Here an American destroyer approaches a Soviet freighter to check on missilelike shapes on the deck. The American captain soon saw that the objects were not missiles, and left without boarding the Soviet ship.

world, while the Soviet Union was far from prosperous and was a tightly controlled dictatorship. Paradoxically, thus, American support for corrupt regimes, often against legitimate revolutionary movements, betrayed its own revolutionary and democratic heritage and cost the United States much international goodwill.

CHAPTER V

The Tragedy of Vietnam

As negotiations to end the Korean War wound down in 1953, Americans had become committed to containing communism. China was now firmly controlled by the Communists under Mao Zedong. Jiang Jieshi's Nationalists had taken over Taiwan, and with American help were building an island fortress there. The Chinese Communists on the mainland insisted that Taiwan was part of China and ought to be under their control, but the United States made it clear that it would help defend Taiwan if the Communists attacked. At times over the years Communist China made threatening gestures toward Taiwan, but never attacked, fearful of American intervention: The island remained a point of contention into the twenty-first century.

The People's Republic of China and the USSR, which shared a common boundary of more than two thousand miles, were often at odds with each other over various matters, but generally maintained an uneasy alliance. Elsewhere in the Pacific region, as a result of World War II, many countries had thrown off the old European colonial masters and were forming their own governments. One such country was Vietnam, which had been part of French Indochina. Under the determined leadership of Ho Chi Minh, who had lived in both the Soviet Union and China and, as long ago as the peace talks in Versailles in 1918, had pled the cause for Vietnamese independence, the Vietnamese had fought the French masters to a standstill. Because the United States needed the cooperation of France in Europe, Eisenhower extended material aid to them in Vietnam. Nevertheless, in 1954 the French lost a major battle at the city of Dien Bien Phu. A peace treaty was arranged. Vietnam would be divided at the 17th parallel, with a French puppet government to hold the southern part; Ho Chi Minh's group, the northern part. Neither section was to allow foreign forces on its soil, and elections were to be held to choose a new government for a unified Vietnam.

The United States supported the puppet government of South Vietnam against the Communist north, of course. But the South Vietnamese government was corrupt and inefficient. Bribery was usual, and in some cases South Vietnamese officials were selling for their own profit supplies sent by the United States. In 1960 there emerged in South Vietnam a rebel group known as the Vietcong. With help from Ho Chi Minh's North Vietnam, it began to gather supporters.

Ho Chi Minh, the leader of North Vietnam, looked like a quiet and dignified scholar, but he was tough, ruthless, and determined that his country would win in its struggle against a sequence of foreign powers.

Here seemed to be a classic example of what George Kennan, in forging the policy of containment, had called "Russian expansive tendencies." American officials began to talk about the "domino effect"—if Vietnam went communist, nearby nations, like Laos and Cambodia might also fall. Once again there was a misperception: While it was true that the Soviet Union and Communist China were aiding both North Vietnam and the Vietcong rebels in South Vietnam, there is no evidence that communism in Vietnam was under the control of the Soviet Union. Once again, it was a case of local peoples turning to communism in order to throw off despots. But American officials (and many American citizens), by now thoroughly anti-Communist in outlook, saw the hand of the Soviets behind everything and were determined to resist.

Thus began the tragedy of the Vietnam War, surely one of the biggest mistakes the United States government has ever made. The war killed several million people, badly damaged the American economy because of its cost, drastically lowered American prestige around the world, destroyed the careers of two American presidents along with other officials, divided the United States into two camps, and left it with a psychological hangover that lasted for two generations. How did a nation that is supposed to be dedicated to peace and honor get into so terrible and destructive a war?

There are a number of reasons—the American containment policy, the American belief that any war for national liberation was Communist inspired. But unquestionably, the important factor was the pride of presidents: None of the presidents involved—John F. Kennedy, Lyndon B. Johnson, and Richard M. Nixon—wanted to appear "soft on communism"; none wanted to be "the first president to lose a war." They had all seen President Truman vilified for "losing" China to the Communists, and they had seen McCarthyism destroy people's careers. Above all, they wanted to appear firm in the face of a supposed communist threat to American interests. These interests, beyond the unlikely potential of the domino effect, included the area's potential as a site for naval bases and as an economic partner of Japan, which the United States was helping to rebuild. But these were not really *vital* interests.

President Eisenhower had originally decided to support the South Vietnamese government with military supplies. Although Eisenhower felt that the United States ought not to get into a land war in the Asian jungles, he nonetheless warned incoming President John Kennedy about the Communist danger in Vietnam. Once in office, Kennedy, embarrassed by the Bay of Pigs disaster and fearful of appearing soft on communism, soon stepped up the aid to South Vietnam. Fatefully, he also sent in a small number of "advisers," to help the South Vietnamese to fight the rebellious Vietcong. By the end of 1961 the United States had over 3,000 soldiers in Vietnam; by the end of 1963 there were 16,700, and some 600 of them had already died. Although most Americans still were not aware of it, their country was at war.

It was a hard and dirty war. The soldiers suffered from baking heat, tropical humidity, tropical diseases, biting insects, and always the fear of stepping on a mutilating booby trap or a sniper shot coming at them from out of the jungle.

In the fall of 1963, President Kennedy was assassinated. (We discuss the Kennedy assassination in the volume in this series called *The Politics of Prosperity, 1945–2000*.) Kennedy's vice president was Lyndon Johnson, a big, dynamic Texan who had been a powerful politician. Born to a relatively poor family, Johnson was determined to succeed. He worked his way through college, went into politics, and eventually became the majority leader of the Senate. He was known for his domineering personality and his ability to manipulate the people around him to get his way, often in the interest of sound projects. Now, as president, he, too, did not want to appear soft on communism, or lose a war. He was determined to win in Vietnam.

To this point, the Congress had never officially declared war, although

The war in Vietnam was tough and dirty. The soldiers struggled against jungle, heat, insects, and disease. In this combat artist's picture, two soldiers fight their way through a swamp, always aware that a hidden enemy was about to pounce.

it had continued to vote money for the fighting. Johnson wanted the support of Congress, and in August 1964 he used a small-scale attack by the North Vietnamese on American ships in the Gulf of Tonkin as an excuse to push through Congress a resolution supporting the war, which became known as the Gulf of Tonkin Resolution. In fact, Johnson had misled both the Congress and the American public about the seriousness of the

Tonkin attack, but the bill passed overwhelmingly. Congress, many later felt, had abandoned its responsibility to examine the need for the war.

Johnson, having finished out Kennedy's term, was reelected in 1964. By then there were 23,000 American soldiers in Vietnam. The United States was now also attacking North Vietnam with offshore boat patrols and saboteurs because of its support of the Vietcong fighting in South Vietnam. The problem was that no matter what the Americans did, the Vietcong continued to fight. Long before, Ho Chi Minh had told the French that they could kill ten Vietnamese for every Frenchman who died, and he would still win. That still appeared to be so. The Vietcong would attack an American strong point and then melt back into the jungle. In desperation, in March 1965, President Johnson began to bomb North Vietnam heavily. More troops were sent in: by mid-1965 there were 80,000 Americans in Vietnam, and the military was asking for 100,000 more.

Up to this point the American people had paid relatively little attention to the fighting in this strange, faraway place, although at least a few had been worried about American involvement there as far back as the late 1950s. Now Americans began to take a look, and many did not like what they saw. It is often said that the antiwar movement was largely made up of college students who did not wish to kill, or be killed, for a cause they did not agree with. And certainly students, with their chants and parades, were the most visible part of the movement. But it is also true that a great many other people opposed the war, as well. Among them were people in the government itself. One of these was State Department official George Ball, who advised Johnson to get out. Johnson replied that if the United States simply pulled out, the rest of the world would conclude that the nation was only a "paper tiger." Ball answered, "The worst blow would be that the mightiest power on earth is unable to defeat a handful of guerrillas." His words were prophetic.

Johnson still had the support of many citizens and people in government. The military, in particular, kept insisting that it could win if it were given enough troops and planes and bombs. By 1969 there were over a half-million American soldiers in Vietnam. The war had become even nastier. American troops were spraying a substance called Agent Orange over the jungle to cause the foliage to wither, revealing Vietcong soldiers. Napalm, a fiery paste which stuck to people and burned them to death, was used against soldiers and civilians alike.

Sometimes Vietcong guerrillas disguised themselves as peasant farmers, then suddenly produced machine guns and attacked passing American troops. Occasionally, even children would suddenly produce weapons. American soldiers grew suspicious of all Vietnamese, and at times attacked innocent civilians. The best-known of these attacks occurred in March 1968, when a platoon led by Lieutenant William Calley deliberately slaughtered most of the women and children in the village of My Lai in revenge for the killing by the Vietcong of a popular officer.

Not only were the American people growing sick of the slaughter in Vietnam; the morale of the troops there was breaking down. Day after day, in intense heat and humidity, struggling through swamps and minefields under constant sniper fire, they saw their buddies die. They felt they were trapped, and that they, too, might die in a pointless war which no longer had the support of the people back home. A lot of soldiers took drugs, which were easily available in Vietnam's cities. In some cases soldiers killed their own officers who they felt were risking them unnecessarily.

Back home the clamor of dissent was growing. In 1967, 300,000 demonstrators marched in New York City. Later in the same year 100,000 surrounded the Pentagon. Prominent people, like the famous baby doctor Benjamin Spock spoke out against the war.

Then, in 1968, on the eve of the Vietnamese Lunar New Year celebration called Tet, the Vietcong mounted a sudden offensive against

American and South Vietnamese strong points all over the country. The Vietcong actually blasted their way into the United States Embassy compound, killing some Americans before they themselves were killed.

Initially the Tet offensive was a success for the Vietcong, but very quickly the Americans and South Vietnamese struck back and drove the Vietcong out. But the Tet offensive was a moral victory for the Vietcong, showing that after years of fighting they still had the ability to inflict real damage on the Americans. Back home the Tet offensive convinced people that the war might drag on indefinitely. The media began to cover the war more fully: Now every night Americans were seeing on television pictures of death and destruction in Vietnam. Soon a majority of Americans disapproved of the war. Tired and discouraged, President Johnson announced that he would not run for another term. At the same time, he stepped up efforts to find peace terms with North Vietnam. And in the fall of 1968 an agreement was reached.

Lyndon Johnson inherited the Vietnam War from his predecessors, and was determined not to lose it. He increased American troops there again and again. As the death tolls mounted, Americans turned against the war, and Johnson, whose domestic programs are still much admired, was forced to give up running for another term.

This combat artist's drawing, entitled Race Against Death, *shows soldiers carrying a wounded comrade into a medical station.*

However, that fall Richard Nixon was running for the presidency against Johnson's vice president, Hubert Humphrey. Critics have claimed, and some historians agree, that Nixon, fearful that Johnson would promote Humphrey's campaign by pulling an "October surprise" by signing a peace treaty, secretly persuaded the South Vietnamese leaders to disavow Johnson's proposals, with the claim that Nixon could get better terms for them if he won the election. For whatever reasons, the peace deal collapsed. Nixon won the election.

While it is true that morale among American soldiers was low at times, it is also true that the Vietnam War produced its share of heroes. One of them, Chief Warrant Officer Fred Ferguson, was pilot of a "Huey" helicopter. Helicopters had been used in the Korean War, but they became an essential tool in Vietnam. Heavily armed with machine guns and rocket launchers, they could be quickly brought in to attack concentrations of enemy troops, deliver ground troops, remove the

Huey helicopters came into their own in Vietnam. The war was fluid, with battles suddenly breaking out here and there in the jungle. Helicopters allowed American troops to move quickly in and out of the fighting.

wounded, provide eyes for troops fighting blindly in the jungles, and bring out surprised and outnumbered American patrols. But, flying low, helicopters were easy targets for the enemy: Six thousand pilots and crewmen were killed in Vietnam.

During the Tet offensive Fred Ferguson learned about a helicopter crew downed near Hue. They had managed to get inside an American compound that was desperately fighting off a large force of the enemy. Ferguson thought, "If I was there, I'd want someone to get me out." Covered by three other gunships, he flew toward the compound through a deadly rain of enemy fire, his chopper taking several hits. Over the compound, he discovered only a tiny space available for landing. With great skill he set the chopper down. The crew in the compound leapt aboard with mortar shells falling all around them. As the chopper rose, a mortar hit, shaking the airship violently. By the time he got back to his base, Ferguson said, "The helicopter was coming apart. It was shaking so bad I couldn't read the instruments." But he had saved the men. Heroes like Fred Ferguson were not in short supply in Vietnam.

Back in Washington, the new president, Richard Nixon, knew that he had to get the United States out of Vietnam. The prestige of the United States around the world had suffered badly. Few people anywhere thought that America had any right to be meddling in Vietnam, and the deaths of so many women and children seemed particularly immoral. Many Americans felt the same way. But, like the presidents before him, Nixon did not want to lose a war.

President Nixon sent his assistant for national security, and later secretary of state, Henry Kissinger, to Paris to hold secret talks with the North Vietnamese. Kissinger was a wily diplomat who believed that nations always did—and should do—what was in their best interests, regardless of morality.

Meanwhile, Nixon had actually expanded the war into neighboring Cambodia, from where the Vietcong was mounting attacks. Nixon's plan was "Vietnamization"; that is, American troops would be withdrawn and South Vietnamese forces would be substantially bolstered. In addition, Nixon secretly promised the South Vietnamese that he

Henry Kissinger, President Nixon's primary foreign policy adviser, was shrewd and realistic. He accepted the idea that governments must often do unpleasant things for the good of their countries. He was important in molding Nixon's policy in Vietnam.

would respond "with full force" if North Vietnam broke the agreement.

Nixon then mounted a great air attack against North Vietnam, which killed at least 2,000 civilians. People around the world were horrified, but Nixon would not back down, saying that he would end the bombing if the North Vietnamese would negotiate seriously. In January 1973 an agreement was reached: The United States would quickly leave Vietnam, and there would be a cease-fire supervised by an international commission. These terms were very similar to the ones Johnson had agreed to in 1968; Since then 20,000 more Americans, and many more Vietnamese, had died. Nixon did not expect the North Vietnamese to abide by the cease-fire, but he hoped that the South Vietnamese forces were now strong enough to hold them off.

They were not. By March 1973, American troops were gone. Some South Vietnamese troops fought well, but others did not. As the North Vietnamese and the Vietcong pressed forward, the South Vietnam government, always unstable, lost control of the situation. In the spring of 1975, North Vietnamese troops poured into the South Vietnam capital, Saigon. American airplanes evacuated Americans and as many South Vietnamese as they could, with the last Americans taken out by helicopter from the roof of the Embassy. The war was over. It cost over three million Vietnamese lives, millions more in Cambodia and Laos; hundreds of thousands maimed; ten million or more refugees; and about 58,000 American military killed and as much as 300 billion of American taxpayer dollars.

How could the world's mightiest power have fallen before an undersupplied army of guerrillas? In part, it was because nuclear weapons, missiles, and advanced airplanes are not much use in a jungle war. In part, it was because the United States dared not do what it might have done to win—invade North Vietnam itself: At that point the Chinese might have come in, as they had in Korea. But mainly the war was lost because the American people refused to support it. Indeed, by 1973 the

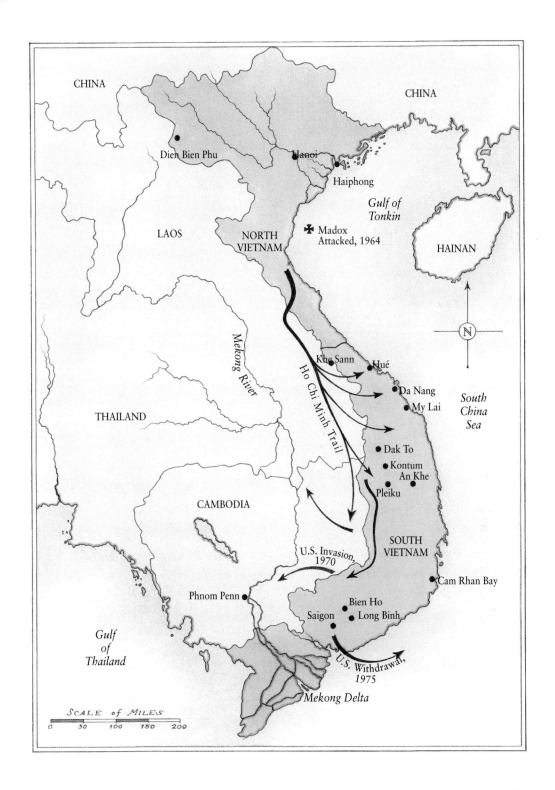

CHINA

CHINA

Dien Bien Phu

Hanoi

Haiphong

*Gulf of
Tonkin*

LAOS

NORTH
VIETNAM

✝ Madox
Attacked, 1964

HAINAN

N

Mekong River

Khe Sann

Hué

Da Nang

My Lai

*South
China
Sea*

THAILAND

Dak To

Kontum
An Khe

Pleiku

Ho Chi Minh Trail

CAMBODIA

SOUTH
VIETNAM

U.S. Invasion,
1970

Cam Rhan Bay

Phnom Penn

Bien Ho

Saigon   Long Binh

*Gulf
of
Thailand*

U.S. Withdrawal,
1975

Mekong Delta

SCALE of MILES

0   50   100   150   200

Unhappily, tens of thousands of civilians were killed and wounded in Vietnam, usually simply as a by-product of the fighting, but in some cases deliberately. In this combat artist's painting two Vietnamese women look at the body of a child killed by an explosive.

Congress was pressing President Nixon to end the war, and the next year began to cut back funds for it.

And what of Nixon's pledge to help South Vietnam "with full force"? By 1973 he was embroiled in the Watergate scandal, which was taking his attention, and by 1974 he was gone. His successor, President Gerald Ford, wisely decided to stay out of Vietnam, and refused to honor the pledge. (For the story of Watergate, see the volume in this series called *The Politics of Prosperity, 1945–2000.*)

The great irony is that twenty-five years later, another president signed a trade agreement with Communist Vietnam, and tourists were signing up for vacation trips to that country. There even seemed some hope that Vietnam might eventually follow other former Communist countries into capitalist democracy.

CHAPTER VI

The Cold War Ends

The Vietnam War left the United States with its prestige, both at home and abroad, sadly diminished. Americans had usually felt that theirs was one of the most moral of nations, a supporter of peace and prosperity for all. They no longer believed it, and the psychological hangover would prove long-lasting. As they discovered that their presidents had lied to them about what they had been doing in Vietnam, they grew cynical; many Americans continued for some time to see the national government as their enemy, rather than as a friend. Furthermore, except for small short-lived operations in Lebanon and Grenada during Ronald Reagan's presidency, for fifteen years after the war they would simply not approve of the sending of troops to fight in foreign nations. Not until the Persian Gulf War of 1990—when President George Bush sent troops and planes to Saudi Arabia after Iraq's invasion of Kuwait, which threatened American oil supplies—was a president able to mount a significant fight anywhere.

Nonetheless, the United States remained one of the world's two superpowers. Both America and the USSR continued the arms race, building ever deadlier missiles with more powerful nuclear warheads.

This picture by a combat artist was called Body Count. *With the war so fluid and difficult to assess, the American officials began to offer reporters the number of bodies of Vietnamese soldiers left after a battle, in order to show that the United States was winning. To many people, the counting of bodies was about all the nation had to show for its long involvement in Vietnam.*

Money being spent on arms could not go for new schools, new housing, and much else. The Soviet Union, which had never developed as large and efficient an industrial system as the United States, was particularly hurt by money spent on arms.

Leaving aside the question of a possible nuclear holocaust, both nations wanted a slowing of the arms race. There began a period now called *détente,* a French word meaning the reduction of tensions. Negotiations for an end to the arms race began. The negotiations were complex, thorny, and involved many technical matters. But in the end some progress was made, and in 1972 President Nixon and Soviet Premier Leonid Brezhnev signed the Strategic Arms Limitation Treaty, known as SALT I. But the treaty still left the superpowers with huge stockpiles of nuclear weapons, and more being made. A second round of negotiations, known as SALT II, began.

Then, in 1975, thirty-five nations met in Helsinki, Finland, and signed a treaty officially ending World War II thirty years after the fighting had stopped. The agreement, called the Helsinki Accords, acknowledged the then-existing situation in Eastern Europe, with the Soviet Union in control of many countries there. In exchange, the Soviets agreed to allow greater freedoms for its citizens. Although the Soviets ignored this part of the Helsinki Accords, it nevertheless encouraged dissidents in the Communist nations to demand human rights.

In June 1979, the SALT II agreement was signed by the new American president Jimmy Carter and Brezhnev, which—generally speaking—allowed each country equality in nuclear weapons. The balance of terror remained, but at least SALT II was a step toward ending it.

But a new problem arose. Some scientists began claiming that it was possible to build *antiballistic* missiles (ABMs), which could shoot down attacking missiles before they landed. If one nation got such a system, it could safely bomb the other, knowing that it could shoot down the missiles the other nation sent in retaliation. The balance of terror would be upset. Some Americans wanted to try to build ABMs; the Soviets objected, not sure they could do it, and loath to spend the money anyway. At the beginning of the twenty-first century doubts that the ABMs would work remained; they certainly would not have worked in 1979. Still, the idea that they might hindered further SALT talks.

In December 1979 the Soviets invaded neighboring Afghanistan to protect a Soviet-backed government in danger of being over-thrown by local missiles. This invasion was contrary to the unspoken agreement that the USSR would not make new conquests. President Carter held back the SALT treaty, halted the sale of wheat to the USSR and refused to let Americans go to Moscow for the 1980 Olympics, to the great unhappiness of hundreds of athletes who had trained for years for the event.

Détente was now over. In 1980 Americans elected as president

Ronald Reagan, who was strongly anti-Communist. President Reagan tended to think in bold strokes, and was not always aware of nuances. He announced that the Soviet Union was an "evil empire," and got Congress to substantially increase the defense budget. He also was prepared to support anticommunist groups around the world. This led the Reagan administration to engage in a dubious operation known today as Iran-Contra. In this plan, American arms were illegally and secretly sold to Iran, and the profits illegally given to the *Contras* in Nicaragua, who, with American support, were fighting the left-wing government there. President Reagan's defenders say Iran-Contra was the work of people lower down in the government, but the record seems to show that Reagan knew and approved of the operation. Many of his officials were eventually indicted for crimes committed in the affair but Reagan was never charged. America, it appeared to many people, was now doing things that were immoral and often illegal in the name of fighting communism. The Cold War was on again.

But back in the Soviet Union troubles were piling up. With huge sums being spent on the military, there were great shortages of civilian goods. Even in Moscow whole families typically lived in two- and three-room apartments. In the food stores, there might be plenty of butter one day, but no sausages; plenty of sausages the next day, but no fresh fruit. Few people had cars, heating fuel was often short, clothes were shoddy and ill-fitting. Many of the Soviet people resorted to vodka for solace; alcoholism was a serious problem, and morale was low.

In 1985 a new, younger leader, Mikhail Gorbachev, took over. Gorbachev did not intend to bring about radical changes, but he recognized that unless military spending was reduced, none of the other problems could be solved. Among other things, he saw that capitalism was not about to collapse; instead, Communism was in danger. The two systems would have to "co-exist."

Summit meetings between Reagan and Gorbachev were arranged.

Soviet premier Gorbachev, shown here with President Reagan, did not intend to bring about sweeping changes to the Soviet Union, but he recognized that change had to come. Once he opened the doors, events got away from him.

Surprisingly, Ronald Reagan, for all his thunderings about the evil empire, began to agree that the two systems could live together. He tended to think in terms of personalities, rather than ideas, and took to the warm, outgoing Gorbachev. Some progress was made toward getting rid of nuclear weapons.

In the Soviet Union, Gorbachev introduced the idea of *glasnost,* or openness: People would be more free to criticize the government. He also allowed elections for certain officials. Whatever Gorbachev intended, he found himself mounted on a horse that was going in its own direction.

Then in 1989 came the critical step. Gorbachev decided that he had to let the captive nations in East Europe go. The Soviet Union could no longer afford to keep troops in those countries. Perhaps more important, Gorbachev had come to realize that there was something wrong with the Soviet system if people could only be held to it by force. He announced that he would not use troops to keep these Communist governments in office in East Europe. Within weeks the people in Poland and Hungary had put in new, more democratic governments. Soon East Germany, Romania, Bulgaria, and Czechoslovakia joined the parade. Symbolically,

As it became clear that the Soviet Union was in turmoil, East Berliners began crossing over the wall into West Berlin. When they realized that nobody was stopping them, they started to pull down the wall dividing the old German capital city.

the great event was the pulling down of the wall dividing East and West Berlin. On the night of November 9, 1989, the East Berlin government announced that East Berliners were free to travel to West Berlin. At midnight thousands danced on the wall, as hundreds of thousands crossed into West Berlin. Soon the wall itself was being pulled down. With shocking suddenness, the Cold War, which had dominated world politics for nearly half a century, was over. In 1990 East and West were reunited into a new democratic Germany.

What was good for the captive nations had to be good for the USSR itself. It rapidly disintegrated into fifteen independent states, such as the Ukraine, Estonia, and Georgia. These former Soviets were slow to stabilize. Their economies remained poor, and progress toward democracy was painfully slow and sometimes set back. Russia itself remained the

The Breakup of the Soviet Union
1990–1991

dominant power, but at times it verged on chaos, with gangsters running many businesses, and much corruption and bribery everywhere. But still, progress toward democracy went slowly forward.

Why did the Soviet Union collapse so swiftly? In part it was due to the pressure of the Cold War itself, which required those enormous expenditures for military power. The Soviet industrial machine was simply not capable of producing as much as the American one did. The economy of a huge nation of more than 2.5 billion people could not be run efficiently by one central bureaucracy located in Moscow. Most Socialist nations nationalized only the most basic industries like transportation and energy production and left the rest to the forces of the marketplace. The Soviets tried to run the whole thing. In addition planners in Moscow often let political concerns get in the way of efficiency; a certain factory head, or the chief of a local area, might have to be given favors when a factory located elsewhere might have done the job better. Inevitably, there

By 1991 Boris Yeltsin had taken over from Gorbachev. He was an erratic man often plagued by bad health, but he allowed many kinds of freedoms that had not existed in Russia and its satellite nations for decades.

were constant payments of bribes. Finally, under Soviet communism few people worked their hardest. Nobody could be fired—everybody was guaranteed a job; on the other hand, most workers could not get raises or advance in their industries. There was no reason for anyone to put real effort into the job, and they didn't. The long-standing joke in the Soviet Union was, "We pretend to work and they pretend to pay us."

Yet another reason for the Soviet collapse was that although under communism everybody was supposed to be on an equal level, in practice officials always managed to live very well indeed—have big apartments, summer homes, big cars, plenty of food—while everybody else struggled.

The ideals of the early communist leaders were long gone. The people could see this, and they were bitter about it.

Finally, the prosperity of the Western democracies, especially the United States, was the envy of people in the communist nations. Communist leaders tried to keep their people from knowing about the wealth of the Western nations, but Western magazines, books, and television shows were constantly smuggled in. People in the Communist nations—living in tiny apartments with no cars; only small black-and-white television sets showing government-approved shows; standing in line for hours in shops to buy basic foods—were stunned by the cars, homes, food, and clothing enjoyed by ordinary working people in the West. By 1960 or so, the Soviet people were tired of Communism.

To be sure, the best society is not necessarily the one that produces the most things. Human life is not just about television sets, luxurious cars, and large houses with private swimming pools. Having good relationships with healthy, happy friends and family, working at interesting jobs, and having spare time for hobbies, most people would agree, matter more. Nonetheless, people do want to be prosperous, to have available to them a wide variety of products to choose from. The Western democracies provided this; the communist nations did not.

Perhaps most important, the nature of capitalism had changed, at least in some respects. Communism had arisen in the nineteenth century in response to the plight of millions of working people who labored long hours for meager wages and lived in woeful conditions. Throughout the twentieth century, people in democracies, often with much struggle, through unions and the power of the vote, got wages raised, hours shortened, working conditions improved.

Although economic inequality remains a prominent characteristic of American society, with far too many families too poor to live adequately, American-style capitalism has delivered much of what Soviet-style communism only promised.

BIBLIOGRAPHY

For Students:

Dudley, William. *The Vietnam War: Opposing Viewpoints.* San Diego, CA: Greenhaven, 1990.

Eskow, Dennis. *Lyndon Baines Johnson.* New York: Franklin Watts, 1993.

Finkelstein, Norman H. *Thirteen Days, Ninety Miles: The Cuban Missile Crisis.* New York: Julian Messner, 1994.

Harrison, Barbara, and Daniel Terris. *A Twilight Struggle: The Life of John Fitzgerald Kennedy.* New York: Lothrop, Lee and Shepard, 1992.

Jacobs, William Jay. *Search for Peace: The Story of the United Nations.* New York: Atheneum, 1996.

Kort, Michael G. *The Cold War.* Brookfield, CT: Millbrook Press, 1994.

Larsen, Rebecca. *Richard Nixon: Rise and Fall of a President.* New York: Franklin Watts, 1991.

Lubetkin, Wendy. *George Marshall.* New York: Chelsea House, 1989.

Marrin, Albert. *America and Vietnam: The Elephant and the Tiger.* New York: Viking, 1992.

Morris, Jeffrey. *The Truman Way.* Minneapolis, MN: Lerner, 1995.

Myers, Walter Dean. *A Place Called Heartbreak: A Story of Vietnam.* Austin, TX: Raintree/Steck-Vaughn, 1993.

Pietrusza, David. *The End of the Cold War.* San Diego, CA: Lucent, 1995.

Sandberg, Peter Lars. *Dwight D. Eisenhower.* New York: Chelsea House, 1986.

Smith, Carter, ed. *The Korean War.* Englewood Cliffs, NJ: Silver Burdett, 1990.

Stein, Conrad. *The Korean War: "The Forgotten War."* Springfield, NJ: Enslow, 1994.

Summers, Harry G. *Korean War Almanac.* New York: Facts on File, 1990.

Warren, James A. *The Cold War: The American Crusade Against the*

Soviet Union and World Communism, 1945–1990. New York: Lothrop, Lee and Shepard, 1996.

Westerfield, Scott. *The Berlin Airlift.* Englewood Cliffs, NJ: Silver Burdett, 1989.

For Teachers:

Alperovitz, Gar. *The Decision to Use the Atomic Bomb and the Architecture of an American Myth.* New York: A. Knopf, 1995.

Ambrose, Stephen, and Douglas Brinkley. *Rise to Globalism.* 8th ed. New York: Penguin Books, 1997.

Boyer, Paul. *By the Bomb's Early Light: American Thought and Culture at the Dawn of the Atomic Age.* New York: Pantheon, 1985.

Bundy, McGeorge. *Danger and Survival: Choices about the Atom Bomb in the First Fifty Years.* New York: Random House, 1988.

Gaddis, John Lewis. *Strategies of Containment: A Critical Appraisal of Postwar American National Security.* New York: Oxford University Press, 1981.

———. *We Now Know.* New York: Oxford University Press. 1997.

Herring, George C. *America's Longest War: The United States and Vietnam, 1950–1975.* 3rd ed. New York: McGraw Hill, 1996.

Hunt, Michael. *Lyndon Johnson's War: America's Cold War Crusade in Vietnam, 1945–1968.* New York: Hill and Wang, 1996.

Kaufman, Burton I. *The Korean Conflict*. Westport, CT: Greenwood Press, 1999.

Le Feber, Walter. *America, Russia, and the Cold War, 1945–1996*. New York: McGraw Hill, 1997.

Leffler, Melvin. *A Preponderance of Power*. Stanford, CA: Stanford University Press, 1992.

LeoGrande, William M. *Our Own Backyard: The United States in Central America, 1977 to 1992*. Chapel Hill: University of North Carolina Press, 1998.

McMahon, Robert J. *The Limits of Empire: The United States and Asia Since World War II*. New York: Columbia University Press, 1999.

Painter, David S. *The Cold War: An Interdisciplinary History*. New York: Routledge, 1999.

Paterson, Thomas G. *On Every Front: The Making and Unmaking of the Cold War*. New York: W.W. Norton, 1992.

Sherry, Michael S. *In the Shadow of War: The United States since the 1930s*. New Haven, CT: Yale University Press, 1995.

Winkler, Allan M. *The Atom and American Life*. New York: Oxford University Press, 1993.

INDEX

Page numbers for illustrations are in **boldface**

JAMES LINCOLN COLLIER is the author of a number of books both for adults and for young people, including the social history *The Rise of Selfishness in America*. He is also noted for his biographies and historical studies in the field of jazz. Together with his brother, Christopher Collier, he has written a series of award-winning historical novels for children widely used in schools, including the Newbery Honor classic, *My Brother Sam Is Dead*. A graduate of Hamilton College, he lives with his wife in New York City.

CHRISTOPHER COLLIER grew up in Fairfield County, Connecticut and attended public schools there. He graduated from Clark University in Worcester, Massachusetts and earned M.A. and Ph.D. degrees at Columbia University in New York City. After service in the Army and teaching in secondary schools for several years, Mr. Collier began teaching college in 1961. He is now Professor of History at the University of Connecticut and Connecticut State Historian. Mr. Collier has published many scholarly and popular books and articles about Connecticut and American history. With his brother, James, he is the author of nine historical novels for young adults, the best known of which is *My Brother Sam Is Dead*. He lives with his wife Bonnie, a librarian, in Orange, Connecticut.